hton
ı
urt

MW00987019

# READING Adventures

## Welcome, Reader!

In this magazine, you will discover a world of achievers. You'll read about a runner who crossed America in a 1928 foot race and a mountain climber who relies on his sense of touch. A neighborhood that comes together to save a dog may inspire you.

You'll read poems and articles about sports, spellers, and inventions, and you'll do lots of fun activities.

So, on your mark…get set…turn the page!

Jesse Owens, Six World Records

32 USA

"Fast Track" by Nikki Grimes. Copyright © 1999 by Nikki Grimes. Reprinted by permission of Curtis Brown Ltd. "Ode to My Shoes" from *From the Bellybutton of the Moon and Other Summer Poems/ Del ombligo de la luna y otras poemas de verano.* Copyright © 1998 by Francisco X. Alarcón. Reprinted by permission of the publisher, Children's Book Press, San Francisco, CA, www.childrensbookpress.org. "Magnet" from *All The Small Poems and Fourteen More* by Valerie Worth. Text copyright © 1994 by Valerie Worth. Reprinted by permission of Farrar, Straus and Giroux LLC.

"Science Fair Project" from *Almost Late to School and More School Poems* by Carol Diggory Shields. Text copyright © 2003 by Carol Diggory Shields. All rights reserved including the right of reproduction in whole or in part in any form. Reprinted by permission of Dutton Books, a member of Penguin Young Readers Group, a division of Penguin Group (USA) Inc., and Carol Diggory Shields. "I chop chop chop without a stop..." from *Good Sports* by Jack Prelutsky. Text copyright © 2007 by Jack Prelutsky. Reprinted by permission of Alfred A. Knopf, an imprint of Random House Children's Books, a division of Random House, Inc. "Long Jump" from *Swimming Upstream: Middle School Poems* by Kristine O'Connell George. Text copyright © 2002 by Kristine O'Connell George. Reprinted by permission of Houghton Mifflin Harcourt Publishing Company and the author. "Defender" from *Tap Dancing on the Roof: Sijo (Poems)* by Linda Sue Park. Text copyright © 2007 by Linda Sue Park. Reprinted by permission of Houghton Mifflin Harcourt Publishing Company and Curtis Brown Ltd. "Spellbound" from *The Dog Ate My Homework* by Sara Holbrook. Text copyright © 1996 by Sara Holbrook. Reprinted by permission of Boyds Mills Press, Inc. "Company's Coming" from *The Alligator in the Closet and Other Poems Around the House* by David L. Harrison. Text copyright © 2003 by David L. Harrison. Reprinted by permission of Wordsong, a division of Boyds Mills Press Inc.

2014 Edition
Copyright © by Houghton Mifflin Harcourt Publishing Company

All rights reserved. No part of this work may be reproduced or transmitted in any form or by any means, electronic or mechanical, including photocopying or recording, or by any information storage or retrieval system, without the prior written permission of the copyright owner unless such copying is expressly permitted by federal copyright law. Requests for permission to make copies of any part of the work should be addressed to Houghton Mifflin Harcourt Publishing Company, Attn: Contracts, Copyrights, and Licensing, 9400 Southpark Center Loop, Orlando, Florida 32819.

Printed in the U.S.A.

ISBN: 978-0-547-86584-3

11 12 13-0928-21 20 19 18 17 16 15 14

4500477774          C D E F G

If you have received these materials as examination copies free of charge, Houghton Mifflin Harcourt School Publishers retains title to the materials and they may not be resold. Resale of examination copies is strictly prohibited.

Possession of this publication in print format does not entitle users to convert this publication, or any portion of it, into electronic format.

# Unit 6

# Paca and the Beetle

## A Folktale from Brazil

A beautiful red, blue, gold, and green macaw watched a brown beetle as it crawled across the jungle floor.

"Where are you going, my friend?" Macaw called out.

"I am going to the sea."

Just then, a paca skittered by. "You?" Paca laughed. "You're so slow it will take you a hundred years!" Macaw looked down. "You shouldn't brag, Paca. Why don't you race him? I'll give a new coat to whoever first reaches the big tree beside the river."

Paca laughed harder. "This is no race!" he giggled. "You may as well give me the yellow coat and black spots of a jaguar right now!"

"I will race," Beetle said. "If I win, I would like a coat like yours, Macaw."

Paca dashed away. Then he thought, "Why should I hurry? I am so much faster than slow Beetle. I can take my time." He smiled, thinking of the fine new coat he would soon wear.

When Paca neared the tree, however, he was amazed to see Beetle on a branch waiting for him.

Scarlet macaws are found throughout South America. These spectacular birds are about three feet long from head to tail.

4

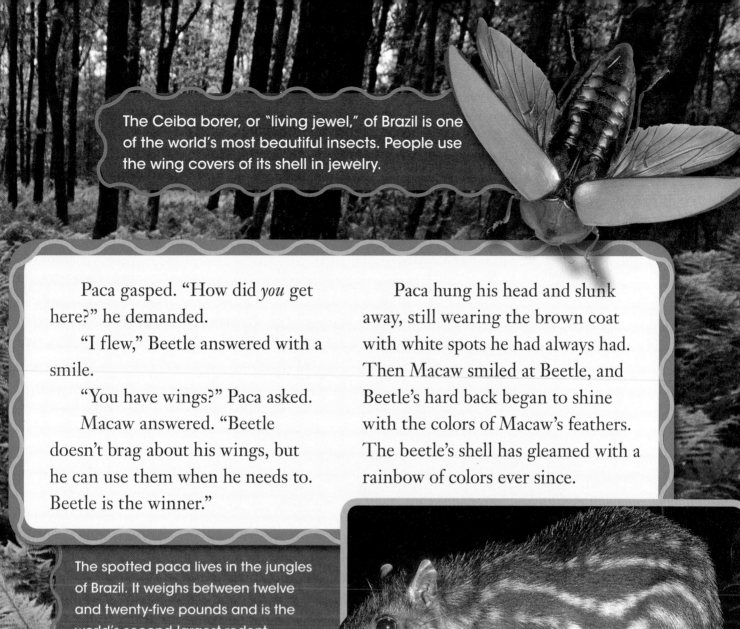

The Ceiba borer, or "living jewel," of Brazil is one of the world's most beautiful insects. People use the wing covers of its shell in jewelry.

Paca gasped. "How did *you* get here?" he demanded.

"I flew," Beetle answered with a smile.

"You have wings?" Paca asked.

Macaw answered. "Beetle doesn't brag about his wings, but he can use them when he needs to. Beetle is the winner."

Paca hung his head and slunk away, still wearing the brown coat with white spots he had always had. Then Macaw smiled at Beetle, and Beetle's hard back began to shine with the colors of Macaw's feathers. The beetle's shell has gleamed with a rainbow of colors ever since.

The spotted paca lives in the jungles of Brazil. It weighs between twelve and twenty-five pounds and is the world's second-largest rodent.

## Discuss the Selection

• What is the moral, or lesson, in this story? Which story details explain this lesson?

• Compare and contrast "Paca and the Beetle" and *The Raven: An Inuit Myth* from Lesson 20. How are the characters, settings, and plots alike and different?

# The Foot Race Across America

**B**ack in 1926, in the hills around Foyil, Oklahoma, the jackrabbits must have gotten used to the sound of Andy Payne running by. The Cherokee teenager was almost as fast as they were.

Andy loved to run. After he finished the morning chores on his family's farm, he ran five miles to school. He often got there before his brothers and sisters, who arrived on horseback. "I just . . . had a knack for being able to cover the ground on foot," he later explained. In those days, Andy won prizes in many track tournaments, especially long-distance events like the mile. His biggest race would be much longer than that, though.

# "Runners Wanted"

After he graduated from high school in 1927, Andy, now age twenty, went to Los Angeles, California, to look for a job. Work turned out to be hard to find. One day he read an ad in a newspaper that would change his life. "Runners wanted," the ad said. An International Trans-Continental Foot Race was going to take place in March. The race would start in Los Angeles and end across the country in New York City. That was a distance of over 3,400 miles. The winner would receive twenty-five thousand dollars!

The 1920s were already known for crazy contests. There were dance marathons, six-day bicycle races, even people setting records for sitting on flagpoles. A man named C. C. Pyle planned the foot race to follow the recently built Route 66, a road that stretched from Los Angeles to Chicago.

Andy Payne was excited. He felt he had as good a chance to win as anyone. The prize money would help his parents pay for their farm. It might also help persuade his girlfriend, Vivian Shaddox, to marry him.

# The Starting Line

Andy hurried back to Oklahoma. He talked his father and local officials into lending him the $125 he needed to enter the race. Then he returned to California to train. After three weeks of running and getting into shape there, he felt ready.

On the morning of March 4, 1928, Andy lined up with nearly two hundred other runners at the starting line. They came from across the United States as well as from other countries, including Finland, Switzerland, Canada, and Italy. They were as young as sixteen and as old as sixty-three. A few were already famous for competing in marathons and other long-distance races. One was the son of a millionaire. Most, however, were poor. In 1928, an average factory worker earned $1,200 a year. Winning the prize money would be like receiving twenty years' salary.

Finally, the great football player "Red" Grange gave the signal. Boom! All 199 men sprang forward, each one dreaming of victory in New York City.

# Over Mountains and Deserts

The first day of the race was the easiest. All the runners made it to the town of Puente, California, seventeen miles away. But it would soon get harder. The runners had to climb steep Cajon (kuh HOHN) Pass, and then deal with the intense heat of the Mojave (moh HAH vay) Desert. By the 12th of March—one week into the race—more than fifty runners had dropped out, tired by the steep climbs and blistered by the desert sun.

A record was kept of the runners' time for each day. Surprising many of the more famous runners was number forty-three, Andy Payne. Andy was running in third place.

As the runners left behind California for Arizona, they faced even tougher climbs. By March 21st, more than half of the original 199 had dropped out, including the man who had been in first place, the South African long-distance champion, Arthur Newton.

The runners had also discovered that C. C. Pyle, the race organizer, was not a man of his word. Instead of the big meals they enjoyed at the start of the race, they were now served poor stews. Often, Pyle's big caravan, nicknamed "America," was late with the tents, cots, and blankets—which were never washed. Then the runners were forced to sleep in barns or stables.

Andy Payne was having his own troubles. He had tonsillitis and a fever. But he kept up the pace. After the runners had made their way through the snow and mud of northern Texas, Andy entered his home state of Oklahoma in the lead.

# The Bunion Derby

By now the foot race was attracting lots of attention. The newspapers had begun to call it "The Bunion Derby." But Andy was lucky—he didn't have bunions, swelling of the big toes. In Oklahoma City, Andy told a cheering crowd and the governor of the state, "Hope to see you in New York." When he ran through his hometown of Foyil, he took a few minutes to visit his girlfriend, Vivian, and his family. And he bought a new pair of running shoes.

Andy was becoming friendly with some of the other runners. One, John Salo, had adopted a dog in Arizona named Blisters, and ran with Blisters all the way to Missouri. Phillip Granville, a Canadian, believed he could win the race by walking, then changed his mind and began to run. Andy's closest friend was also his closest rival, an Englishman named Peter Gavuzzi. They traded the lead from Oklahoma to Ohio. That was where Peter, more than six hours ahead of Andy, had to drop out because of a toothache.

With a thousand miles left to go, Andy Payne took over first place for good.

# The Finish Line

By the third week of May, the runners were closing in on New York City. The daily distances were getting longer. One day, the men ran nearly seventy-five miles. C. C. Pyle, the race organizer, was broke. It wasn't certain that he would be able to pay the winners the prize money. But on May 26, 1928, the Bunioneers, as the fifty-five remaining runners were now called, came plodding in to New York's Madison Square Garden. Even though they had been running for eighty-four days, they had to keep running, circling the arena for another twenty miles before the race was over.

In the end, C. C. Pyle did come up with the money. It took 573 hours, 4 minutes, and 34 seconds, but Andy Payne achieved his dream. He won the $25,000 first prize. John Salo (and Blisters) won the $10,000 second prize. Phillip Granville, the Canadian walker, won the third prize of $5,000.

Andy took the train back to Oklahoma. True to his word, he paid what his family owed on their farm. In 1929, he married Vivian Shaddox. That year there was a second Trans-Continental foot race, this one going in the opposite direction, from New York City to Los Angeles. Andy did not take part. The winner was Peter Gavuzzi, his sore tooth all healed.

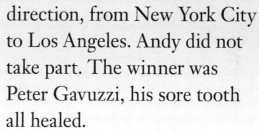

Today, people still remember Andy Payne for his remarkable achievement. Every May an "Andy Payne Bunion Run" marathon takes place in Oklahoma City. And if you happen to be traveling on Route 66 by Andy's hometown of Foyil, you'll see a life-size statue of Andy, doing what he loved to do. Running.

Madison Square Garden occupied this building from 1925 to 1968.

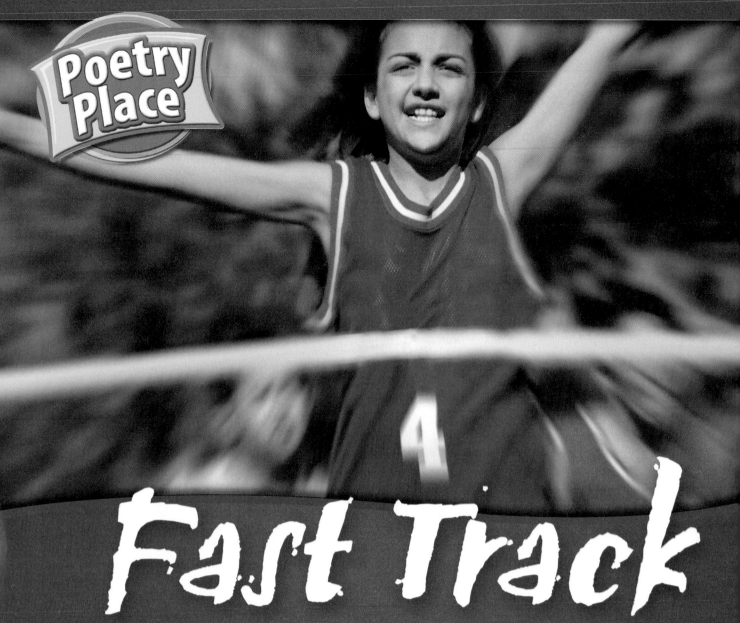

# Fast Track

by Nikki Grimes

When the whistle blows
I am ready and set
and no one can tell me
I am too anything
or less than enough.
I am a tornado of legs and feet
and warm wind whipping past
everyone else on the track
and all that's on my mind
is scissoring through
the finish line.

# Ode to My Shoes

## by Francisco X. Alarcón

my shoes
rest
all night
under my bed

tired
they stretch
and loosen
their laces

wide open
they fall asleep
and dream
of walking

they revisit
the places
they went to
during the day

and wake up
cheerful
relaxed
so soft

**Discuss Poetry**
- The first poet uses a **metaphor**. What does she say a runner *is*? How does this help you imagine what it's like to be the runner?
- The second poet uses **personification**. Which human traits does he give to a pair of shoes? How do they look, act, and feel?

# Design a Stamp

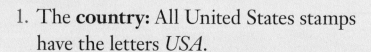

You need a stamp to send a letter. But stamps have another purpose. They are often used to honor people's achievements.

Design a stamp to honor Andy Payne and his race across the United States, or choose another person whose achievement you would like to honor.

Make sure you include the following features in your stamp design:

1. The **country:** All United States stamps have the letters *USA*.

2. The **value:** Include a number that shows how much the stamp costs.

3. A **picture:** Show a picture of the person you are honoring, or show a place or object connected with the achievement.

4. A **name or description:** Include the person's name or a brief description of the achievement. For example, you might use the words *World's fastest runner* for an athlete who set a record.

# Add -ion

When the suffix *-ion* is added to a verb, the new word is a noun. It names the action that the verb shows.

**Example:** Paca didn't **act** kindly toward Beetle. His **action** made him look foolish in the end!

Go on an *-ion* hunt. Read each pair of sentences. Find a word in the first sentence that you can add *-ion* to. Use the noun you form to complete the second sentence on a separate sheet of paper.

1. Do you suggest that we run across the United States? What a silly _____ that is!

2. The runners had nothing to protect them as they ran through the desert. People need _____ from the desert sun.

3. Signs were used to direct the runners. They ran in an east-west _____ across the country.

4. Inspect the map on page 9 to see the race route. During your _____ , count how many states Andy Payne ran through.

5. I predict that you will win a race one day. If my _____ comes true, I'll congratulate you!

RUNNERS: THIS WAY!

# And the

In "Paca and the Beetle," you read about a race between two very different creatures. Write your own story about a contest between two animals that are opposites. For example, the contest might be between the tallest animal and the shortest animal in a jungle. Or the contest might be between the strongest animal and the weakest animal on a farm. Remember, the winner of the contest doesn't have to be the one you'd expect to win.

# Winner Is...

## Story Tips

- Introduce the characters and the setting, or where and when the story takes place.
- Tell about the contest. What is it supposed to prove?
- Describe what happens during the contest.
- Show who wins the contest, and tell why.

# The POWER of Magnets

Chances are there's a magnet on your refrigerator. It's probably holding up a photo, a drawing, or some other piece of paper. Have you noticed that the magnet sticks to the refrigerator but not to the paper? Do you know why?

**This refrigerator magnet is actually pulling on the refrigerator.**

A magnet attracts objects with iron in them. The refrigerator door is probably made of steel, which is made from iron. Paper has no iron in it. That's why the magnet doesn't stick to it.

If you ever spill a box of pins, a good way to pick them up is with a magnet. The magnet will pull the pins toward it. Most of the pins will stick to the ends, or poles, of the magnet. That's because the poles are the most powerful part of a magnet.

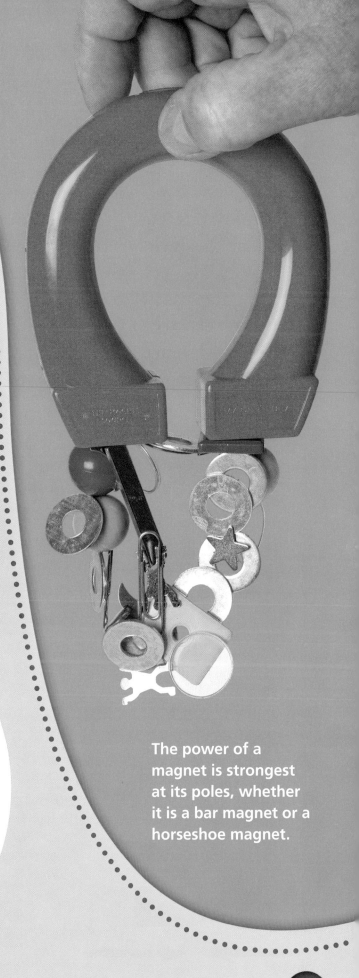

Some magnets are bars. Other magnets are shaped like horseshoes.

The power of a magnet is strongest at its poles, whether it is a bar magnet or a horseshoe magnet.

# Poles and Fields

A magnet has a north pole and a south pole. What happens if you try to touch the north pole of one magnet to the south pole of another magnet? They'll stick together. Opposite poles attract each other.

Will two north poles or two south poles stick together? No, they won't. In fact, they will repel, or push each other away. Like poles repel each other.

This special force that attracts or repels is called magnetic force. A magnet's force is not felt just at its poles. A magnet creates a whole area, or field, of force around it.

Do you want to see a magnetic field? Sprinkle iron filings around a magnet. The iron filings will form a pattern of lines. They show the magnetic field, where the magnet's force works. The lines are closest together at the poles, where the force is strongest.

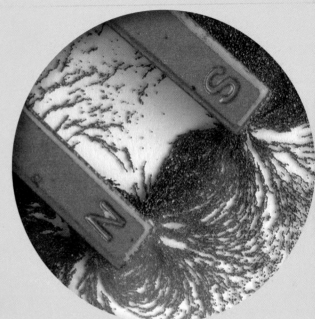

A magnetic field is invisible, but these iron pieces show where it is.

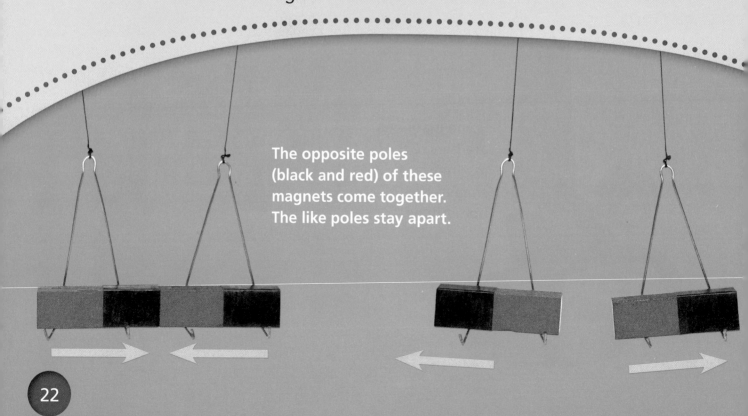

The opposite poles (black and red) of these magnets come together. The like poles stay apart.

# Electromagnets: Turn Them On, Turn Them Off

Some magnets can be turned on and off. If you need a magnet whose force you can control like this, you want an electromagnet. In an electromagnet, wire is wrapped around metal. Electricity can flow through the wire. When you turn the electricity on, the metal becomes a magnet! It is an electromagnet. When you turn the electricity off, the metal stops being a magnet.

Junkyards use huge electromagnets to move old cars. A special crane turns electricity on. That turns a core of metal into a magnet. The car sticks to the magnet, and the crane moves the car with ease. Then the electricity is turned off, and the magnet turns back into plain metal. The car drops into place.

Electromagnets are useful for two reasons: They can be powerful enough to move a car, and they can be turned on and off.

## Michael Faraday's Electric Idea

In 1820, people first learned about electromagnets. That year one scientist saw a magnetic field produced when electricity ran through a metal wire. His observation made another scientist, Michael Faraday, curious. Faraday asked himself: If electricity can produce a magnetic field, can a magnetic field produce electricity?

Faraday tested his idea. In one experiment, he moved a magnet through a coil of wires. Electricity was produced! In another, he moved the coil of wires around a magnet. Again, electricity was produced.

Faraday's work led to two important inventions: the electric generator and the electric motor. The electric generator produces electricity with a magnetic field. The electric motor uses electricity to run things. Now people could use magnets to make electricity do their work for them!

# Electric Generators

*Generate* means "produce or make." An electric generator uses a magnetic field and moving wire coils to produce electricity, just as Michael Faraday discovered.

A power company near your home builds generators. Electricity from these generators comes through power lines into your home. It lets you turn on lights, watch TV, and listen to music. Think of all the times you use electricity. You are using electricity produced in a magnetic field.

Every time you turn on a light switch, electricity comes through a wire. Every time you plug in a cord, electricity comes through the wire. Remember, too, that electricity creates a magnetic field. So every time electricity comes through a wire in your home, it produces a magnetic field. How many magnetic fields do you think are in your home?

A magnetic field is inside this huge generator.

# Electric Motors

Some electricity that comes into your home is used to power electric motors. An electric motor uses electricity to run things. When you plug in and turn on a hair dryer or a fan, an electric motor makes it work.

Some electric motors get their power from batteries. When you put a battery in a watch or a CD player, an electric motor makes it work.

Think about all the toys and tools in your home that have electric motors. Inside each electric motor is a magnet and its magnetic field. How many magnetic fields in electric motors do you think are in your home?

Batteries like these give power to electric motors.

Remember that magnets are not just on your refrigerator door. Magnets help provide the power you use every day.

# ELECTRO

You may not know it, but you live with electromagnets all around you. Here are just a few examples.

*Ding-dong!* Pressing a doorbell turns an electromagnet on. The magnet makes a striker or arm move. It hits a bell, and the doorbell rings.

Did you know that electromagnets help you dry your hair? Any machine with an electric motor uses an electromagnet to turn working parts on and off. So a blow dryer, vacuum cleaner, refrigerator, washing machine, and radio all have electromagnets.

# MAGNETS
## AND YOU

**Electromagnets even help you have fun!**

A computer uses electromagnets too. They help store information on the computer's hard drive so you can find it later.

Music pumps out of a stereo's speakers because of electromagnets. Inside, the cone has a coil attached to it. Around that is a magnet. Electricity creates a magnetic field. This vibrates, or shakes, the coil. The cone moves, too. That's what makes the sounds you hear.

# Poetry Place

# Science Fair Project

## by Carol Diggory Shields

**PURPOSE:**
The purpose of my project this year
Is to make my brother disappear.

**HYPOTHESIS:**
The world would be a better place
If my brother vanished without
a trace.

**MATERIALS:**
3 erasers
White-out
Disappearing ink
1 younger brother
1 kitchen sink

**PROCEDURE:**
Chop up the erasers.
Add the white-out and the ink.
Rub it on the brother
While he's standing in the sink.

**RESULTS:**
The kid was disappearing!
I had almost proved my theorem!
When all at once my mom
came home
And made me re-appear him.

**CONCLUSION:**
Experiment a failure.
My brother is still here.
But I'm already planning
For the science fair *next* year.

# magnet

## by Valerie Worth

This small
Flat horseshoe
Is sold for
A toy: we are
Told that it
Will pick up pins
And it does, time
After time; later
It lies about,
Getting its red
Paint chipped, being

Offered pins less
Often, until at
Last we leave it
Alone: then
It leads its own
Life, trading
Secrets with
The North Pole,
Reading
Invisible messages
From the sun.

## Discuss Poetry

Compare and contrast form in these two poems. How does each poet arrange her words? Notice capitalization, punctuation, rhyme, and line breaks.

# Make a Magnet

Amaze your friends! Tell them you can pick up one paper clip with another without clipping them together. It's not magic. It's magnetism!

## Materials

**1 magnet**
**1 large paper clip**
**1 small paper clip**

1. Straighten out the large paper clip. Set it on a table so it's flat.

2. Hold one end of the paper clip down with a fingertip.

3. Hold the magnet in your other hand. Gently, but firmly, slide the magnet along the paper clip from one end to the other. Then lift the magnet up and away from the paper clip.

4. Repeat Step 3 about ten times. Always stroke the magnet in the same direction.

5. Carefully pick up the magnetized paper clip. Use its tip to pick up the small paper clip.

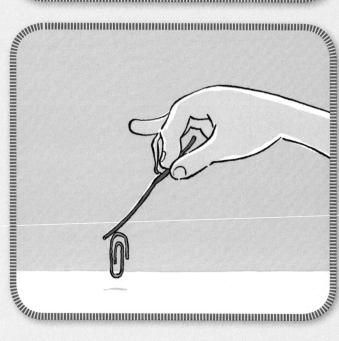

# Do the Magnet Jump

Did you know you can make metal objects "jump"?

1. Tape the ruler onto a table so it won't move.

2. Tape the magnet so one end is facing the beginning of the ruler.

3. Place the pin along the ruler an inch or two away from the magnet. Gently nudge the object toward the magnet until it "jumps" toward the magnet.

4. Record the mark where the object was right before its jump.

5. Repeat Steps 3 and 4 with the other objects. Record the distance each one jumps.

After you do the activity, explain the directions to a classmate.

## Materials
1 ruler
1 magnet
tape
a straight pin
a small and a
large paper clip
a nail

| Object | Distance "Jumped" |
|---|---|
| straight pin | |
| small paper clip | |
| large paper clip | |
| nail | |

# Wow!
## What an Invention!

**Y**ou've been reading about useful inventions—the magnet, the electromagnet, the electric motor, and others. Think about something *you'd* like to invent. What would it do?

Your invention can be simple or complicated. It can be useful or silly. It can even be something that already exists but that you wish you had invented.

Write a description of your invention and what it does. Then draw a picture of it.

## Invention Tips

- State your invention's name.
- Make a drawing of your invention and label its parts.
- Write a description of what your invention does and how it works.

# Becoming ANYTHING He Wants to Be

*I*magine cold *so* cold that bare skin freezes almost instantly. Imagine wind so strong that it could blow you over and deep icy cracks you might fall into at any moment. Now picture a group of mountain climbers making their way through this environment to the highest spot in the world. One of the climbers is Erik Weihenmayer.

On May 25, 2001, Erik did make it to the top of Mount Everest, the tallest mountain on Earth. But Erik could not see the view from the top. He could not even see the snow and ice all around him. He could only feel them because he is blind. Erik is the only blind person ever to reach the top of the world.

On May 25, 2001, Erik became the first blind person to climb to the top of Mount Everest.

## A Hard Beginning

Erik was born with a rare eye disease. He could never see very well. By the time he was 13, the disease had made him blind.

People often think of all the things a blind person can't do because he or she can't see. Erik's father encouraged Erik to think about the things he *could* do. Erik learned that lesson well.

It wasn't always easy. At first, Erik was angry when he lost his sight. He refused to learn Braille, a writing and reading system for blind people. He failed math his first year in high school because he could not read the Braille textbook.

Then Erik started wrestling. It was a sport where his blindness did not slow him. He learned Braille, and his grades improved. He became the captain of the wrestling team. One year he won second place in the state wrestling championship.

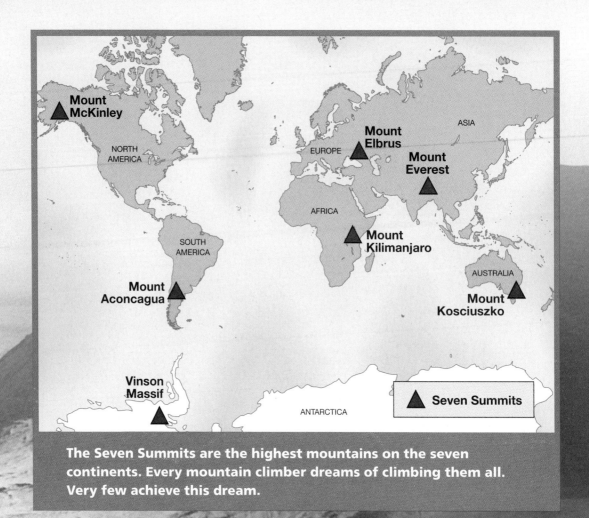

The Seven Summits are the highest mountains on the seven continents. Every mountain climber dreams of climbing them all. Very few achieve this dream.

# The Thrill of the Climb

When he was sixteen, Erik went rock climbing for the first time. The experience changed his life. He loved the feel of the wind and the rock under his hands. Different rocks had different textures. This thrilled him and made him want to climb more and more.

Yet Erik did not want only to follow other climbers. Blind people had climbed that way for a long time. Erik wanted to lead. He wanted to find the toeholds and places for his hands by touch. One night, he proved he *could* lead.

He was climbing with a partner, and they finished after dark. The partner had forgotten his helmet light. He could not see to climb down. But Erik could "see" with his hands. He led the climb back down to safety.

Erik says he loves the beauty of mountain climbing, the movement and the teamwork.

# Climbing the Seven Summits

Soon Erik began climbing mountains! He discovered he could use long poles to lean on and help him feel the ground. He could also use his hearing to sense when a cliff was in front of him, or when the ground dropped off. Sometimes climbers in front of him wore bells or tapped their ice axes against rocks to help direct him.

In 1995, Erik climbed to the top of Denali Peak (Mount McKinley) in Alaska. The TV news reported it: a blind man had climbed the tallest mountain in North America! It was the first of the "Seven Summits" that Erik went on to climb. These mountains are the highest on each of the seven continents. Over the next seven years, Erik climbed them all.

Erik wants other people to think about what they can do and not what they cannot do, just as he has done.

A great athlete, Erik competes in tandem bicycle races. Tandem bikes are for two riders.

## Not Just a World-Class Climber

Erik didn't stop at mountain climbing. At one time he was a teacher and a wrestling coach. He is also a sky diver. He runs marathon races. He skis. He scuba-dives. He does long-distance bike rides. You could never tell Erik that blindness is a handicap.

Now Erik speaks and teaches all around the world. He has written two books. The message in each is that hardships can make us stronger and better people. One of his books is called *Touch the Top of the World*. The story was made into a movie.

Erik also made a movie called *Farther Than the Eye Can See*. It is an adventure film about climbing Mount Everest. Erik used the movie to raise more than half a million dollars for charity. He used his success to help form a group called No Barriers. The group finds ways to help people with disabilities overcome the barriers in their lives.

Today, Erik is trying to help blind people learn to read and write. He wants everyone who cannot see to learn Braille. He speaks all over the world to help make this happen.

Erik was once asked if he believes everything is possible. He answered that there are limits. For example, he cannot drive a car. But, he added, "There are good questions and bad questions in life. The bad questions are what-if questions. 'What if I were smarter, or stronger? What if I could see?' Those are dead-end questions. A good question is, 'How do I do as much as I can with what I have?'"

# My Blue Belt Day!

A karate student shows a roundhouse kick.

## Just What Is Karate?

Karate is an ancient Asian form of self-defense. It uses no weapons. In fact, *karate* in Japanese means "empty hand." In karate, a person uses kicks, punches, blocks, and hand chops to stop an attacker.

Belt colors show how much karate students have learned. Beginners wear white belts. A student must pass a test to achieve each next belt. The kicks and other moves get harder and more complicated with each level of belt. The highest level is the black belt, the sign of the master.

40

## May 3

Why was I so scared this morning? My stomach was doing flips. You'd think I was facing a cougar instead of a karate test!

I didn't feel scared six months ago. That's when I took my test to earn my green belt. I knew the green belt forms and performed all the kicks and blocks and punches just right.

This morning, though, I didn't feel ready for the blue-belt test. I guess I was unsure about my roundhouse kick. The front kick, side kick, and roundhouse kick all need to be perfect to earn the blue belt.

Just before my test, though, my instructor helped me. *Sensei* Scott said I just needed to focus. He said, "Don't think about earning your blue belt. Just think about each move as you do it."

It worked. I snapped my leg into a front kick. I whipped it out into a side kick. Then I shouted "*Yiah!*" and swung my right leg around for a perfect roundhouse kick.

Now I think that in six months I will be trading my blue belt for purple!

**There are different schools of karate.
Most follow this order of belts.**

# I chop chop chop

by Jack Prelutsky

I chop chop chop without a stop,
I move with great agility.
I break a brick with one quick kick—
Karate… that's the sport for me!

# Long Jump

by Kristine O'Connell George

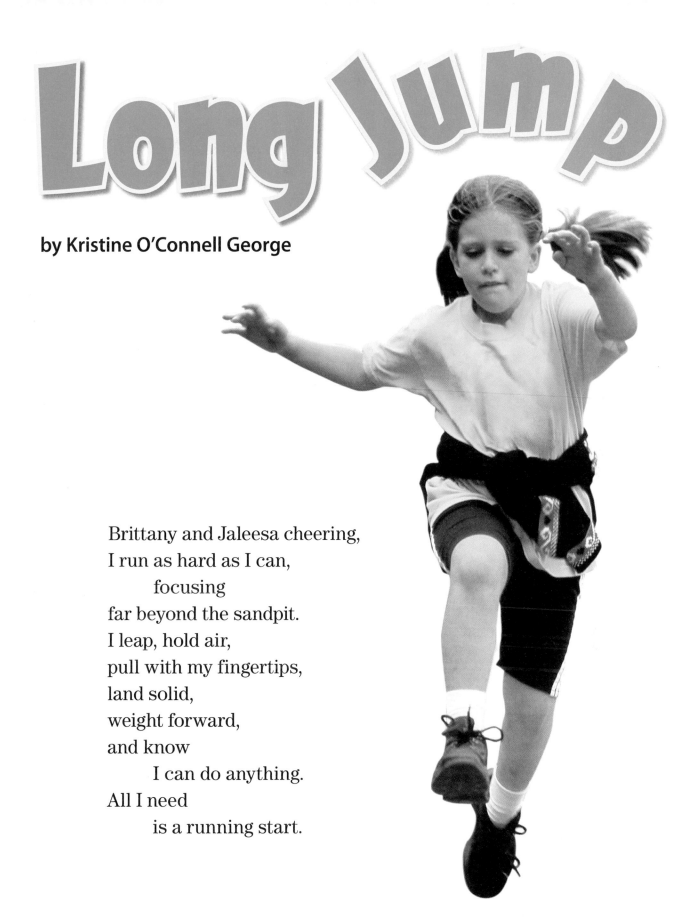

Brittany and Jaleesa cheering,
I run as hard as I can,
        focusing
far beyond the sandpit.
I leap, hold air,
pull with my fingertips,
land solid,
weight forward,
and know
        I can do anything.
All I need
        is a running start.

# Interview an ACHIEVER!

Everyone has done something to be proud of. Maybe it was scoring a winning goal in a game. Maybe it was overcoming a fear. Maybe it was helping someone, or it was learning something new. Whatever it was, it's time to share it.

Interview a classmate about an achievement he or she is proud of. Use the list below to guide your interview. Jot your partner's answers down on a sheet of paper. Using your notes, share your partner's achievement with the rest of your class or group. Be sure to speak clearly and to use correct grammar.

1 Achiever's name
2 What achievement makes you the most proud?
3 When did it happen?
4 Where did it happen?
5 How do you feel about what you did?

# Build a Word

Many English words have word parts called roots from other languages. If you know the meaning of the root, it will help you understand the meaning of the whole word. Here are the meanings of four roots.

| | | | |
|---|---|---|---|
| **auto = self** | **graph = write** | **phon = sound** | **tele = distance** |

**Example:** A **phonograph** is an early record player. It plays **sound** that was **written** down, or recorded, on a disc.

Combine the roots above to make words that answer the riddles below.

**1.** I'm your name that you **write** your**self**. What am I?

**2.** I help you hear **sound** from a **distance**. What am I?

**3.** You use me to **write** a message and send it a **distance**. What am I?

Now make up two words of your own. Use the roots above. Combine them with other words. Your new words do not have to be real. Write a sentence that defines each new word you made.

**Example:** A **telebird** is a bird that flies a long distance.

Answer Key: 1. autograph; 2. telephone; 3. telegraph

45

You read about a man who climbed the highest mountain in the world and a girl who earned her blue belt in karate. You may also have a friend, relative, or classmate who accomplished something great. Or maybe you read a story about a character who does something wonderful.

Choose a real person or a story character who achieved a goal. Write a card, congratulating that person on the achievement.

- Decorate the front of the card.
- Inside, write a message. Tell what you think about the person's achievement, as Carrie has done here. Which sentence tells you her purpose for writing this card?
- Include the date on which you are writing.

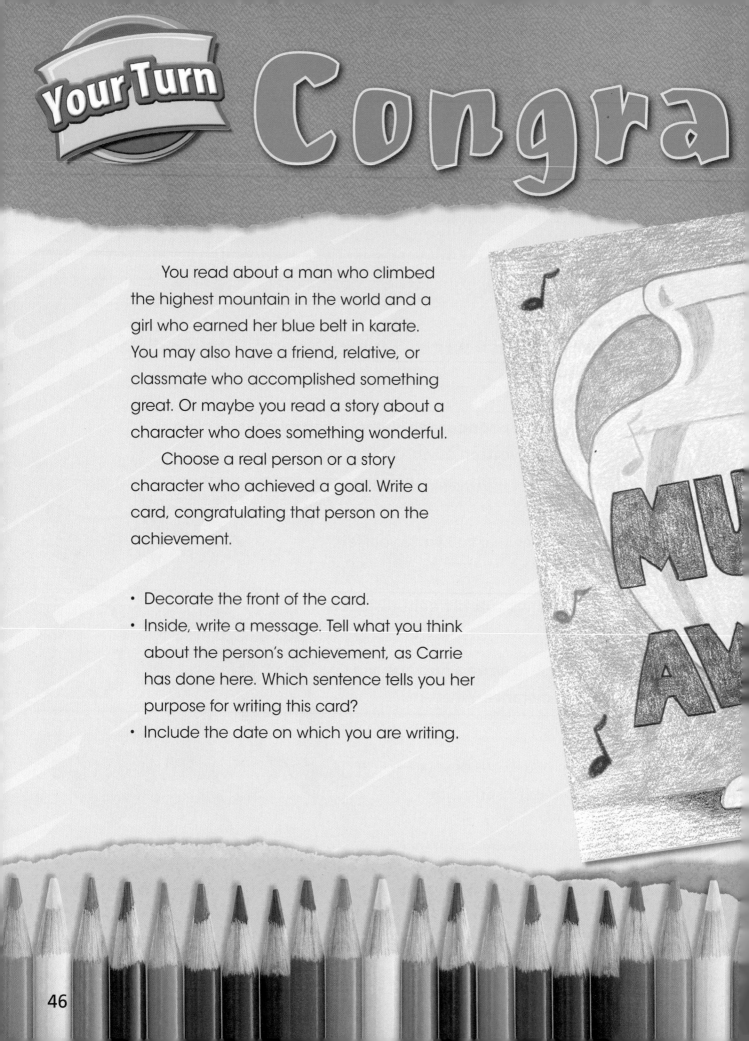

Dear Ava,                     May 1

   I am writing this card to congratulate you on winning the school music award. I know you practiced piano every day, and it showed! Your concert was great. You deserve your award.

              Your friend,

              Carrie

# A New TEAM of HEROES

**Cast of Characters**

Narrator
Lauren
Carla
Hiro
Manny
Gayle

**Narrator:** Lauren, Carla, Hiro, and Gayle are close friends and members of their third-grade soccer team, the Hawks. Of course, as with any team, some players are better than others.

**Lauren:** Look at Carla fly down the field! *She's* the reason we win so many games.

**Hiro:** I wish I could play like her.

**Gayle:** Me too. But it takes *all* of us to win games, not one player.

**Narrator:** Late in the fall, just before a big game, a new player joins the Hawks. The coach introduces Manny to everyone. The four friends hope he knows the game.

**Gayle:** I wonder what kind of player he is.

**Carla:** Do you think he's good?

**Hiro:** Why don't you go ask him?

**Carla:** No, *you* ask!

**Lauren:** It doesn't matter, since we've got Carla on the field! No one can stop you, Carla.

**Carla:** Well, I hope he can play.

**Gayle:** Come on. Let's go practice!

**Narrator:** A few days later is the big game. Before the start, Manny sits on one end of the bench tying his shoes. The group of friends sit at the other end.

**Hiro:** This game will be tough.

**Gayle:** Coach says we can win if we all play hard.

**Lauren:** That new boy is just sitting by himself.

**Carla:** Maybe we should talk to him.

**Gayle:** Let's not worry about it now. It's time for the game to begin.

**Narrator:** As always, Carla runs onto the field, leading her other teammates.

**Hiro, Gayle,** and **Lauren** (together): Go, Carla!

**Narrator:** The game is close. Carla scores two goals, but the other team scores two as well. Every player on the Hawks' bench has had a turn except Manny. When Gayle comes off the field, she decides to sit next to him.

**Gayle:** Your name is Manny, right? I'm Gayle.

**Manny:** Hi. You're not a bad soccer player, Gayle.

**Gayle:** Well, I'm not as good as Carla.

**Manny:** Yes, she's great!

**Narrator:** Hiro and Lauren move down the bench.

**Hiro:** She sure is!

**Narrator:** Just then, the opposing team scores. Everyone on the bench groans.

**Lauren:** How could that happen?

**Hiro:** Now we're losing!

**Manny:** I've noticed something. Their goalie always moves to her left when we're ready to take a shot. I think I could score on her.

**Hiro:** Only Carla can beat their goalie.

**Gayle:** Manny, do you really think you can score on her?

**Narrator:** Manny nods. Gayle leaps up to talk with the coach.

**Lauren:** What makes you so sure you can score, Manny?

**Manny:** I played a lot of soccer at home in Guatemala. I faced goalies like her, and I'm sure I can get past her.

**Narrator:** Just then, Carla comes to the sideline. Her uniform is stained with grass and dirt. She is gasping for breath.

**Carla:** I can hardly run any more. And now we're losing by a goal!

**Gayle:** You'll have some help soon. The coach is going to put Manny in.

**Carla:** I hope you can play well, Manny.

**Manny:** I think I can, and I have an idea. When we attack, drive to the goalie's left, and then pass back across to me. I think the net will be open.

**Carla:** I'll give it a try.

**Lauren:** Well, Coach says I'm going in the game too. Let's do it!

**Narrator:** Manny, Carla, and Lauren race onto the field while the others watch.

**Hiro:** This is amazing! Manny is as good as Carla.

**Gayle:** He might even be better.

**Hiro:** Look at them go!

**Narrator:** On the field, Lauren passes to Carla. Carla races to the goal. The other team's goalie shifts left, just as Manny predicted. Carla passes the ball over to Manny.

**Hiro and Gayle (together):** Goal! Manny scores!

**Narrator:** Manny, Carla, and Lauren run to the sideline during the time out. The grinning players are sweaty and breathing hard.

**Manny:** This time, let's do the same play, but keep running toward the goal, Carla. When they turn to stop me, I'll kick a pass over them back to you.

**Carla:** We'll need to time our passes perfectly.

**Manny:** I can do it. Can you?

**Carla:** I'll try.

**Narrator:** This time, the coach sends Manny, Carla, and Hiro on the field. With just seconds left in the game, Hiro passes the ball to Manny. Their teammates watch as Manny and Carla dash past the bench toward the goal.

**Lauren:** Did you see that pass? Carla is a great player!

**Gayle:** Go, Manny!

**Lauren:** He kicked it across! Get it, Carla!

**Gayle:** She has it! She scores! Goal!

**Lauren** and **Gayle** (together): We win!

**Narrator:** The players start to run off the field. The players on the bench run to meet them.

**Manny:** Great shot, Carla!

**Carla:** Great pass, Manny!

**Hiro:** Three cheers for Carla!

**Lauren:** Three cheers for Manny!

**All:** Three cheers for the HAWKS!

# C-H-A-M

Imagine you are standing on a stage. Hundreds of people in the room are watching you. Millions are seeing you on TV. A man says, "The word is *champion*." It is up to *you* to spell it.

That's how kids in the national spelling bee feel.

Each year, more than 250 kids in elementary and middle school make it to the final bee. They come from all over the United States. A few even come from Canada, the Bahamas, and other countries.

Television helped make spelling bees popular. In 1994, the TV sports station ESPN started showing the national final bee. After that, spelling bees grew fast, and the bees got harder!

To get to the national bee, each speller works up through many smaller bees. A classroom bee might be the first one. The winner then

competes against students from other classrooms in the school. One student will win. That winner will spell against students from other local schools. Finally, the Scripps National Spelling Bee is held in Washington, D.C., and shown on TV.

Getting to the finals is hard work. The ones who make it study and practice day after day. They learn base words and roots. That helps them correctly spell words that they have never even heard before.

The spellers face a lot of pressure. To win, they have to spell harder and harder words. One year, a speller fainted at the microphone. Before anyone could help him, he jumped up and correctly spelled his word!

Another year, Katharine Close won by correctly spelling *ursprache*. Most adults don't even know what that word means. (It means "an early language.") Katharine seemed very cool on TV. She just stood with her hands in her pockets and spelled word after word.

Later, Katharine admitted she was not as cool as she looked. Her hand was in her pocket to hold her good-luck charm. It worked!

**2006:**

When 13-year-old Katharine Close won the national spelling bee in 2006, it was her fifth time in the finals.

# Defender

**By Linda Sue Park**

Everyone wants to get the ball,
run with it, and score a goal.
But when we win one-nothing,
that "nothing" means everything.

It's tough, playing for nothing.
Defense: Intense immense suspense.

# SPELLBOUND

By Sara Holbrook

Confluence

and recompense,

aphid,

ibex,

muse,

chrysalis and zygote.

Words

I know I'll never use.

But like

gossamer and quell,

I had to learn to spell.

# YOU'RE A STAR!

When you reach a goal or do something important, you might receive a Certificate of Achievement.

A certificate is a special award that tells what someone has accomplished. Here's an example:

Certificate Title

Person's Name

Activity

Date

**CERTIFICATE OF ACHIEVEMENT**

Super Speller

This award is presented to

*Noah Lane*

for winning Mesa Elementary School's
Third-Grade Spelling Bee

On this day of *April 8*     Presented by *Anna Day*

Achievement

Signature

Think about the partner you interviewed last week. Reread your interview notes. Use them to make a Certificate of Achievement for your partner. Then give the certificate to your friend.

# Become a Character!

Many characters in stories achieve goals. Think of a character you've read about who is an achiever. It could be one of the soccer players in the magazine article "A New Team of Heroes," or it could be a character in another story you read this year.

Take a sheet of poster board. Cut a hole for your face.

Decorate the board to look like your character. Go before the class and tell your classmates your story:

▸ who you are

▸ what you achieved

▸ how you achieved it

▸ why you are proud of what you did

Be sure to speak clearly while making eye contact with your classmates.

# Extra! Extra!

## Read All About Me!

You've been reading about students who are achievers, including soccer players and spellers.

Now it's your turn!

Think about something you've done that you're proud of, or something you've dreamed of doing. Take the role of a reporter and write a newspaper article that tells the world about your accomplishment.

## Writing Tips

* Start your article by telling what you accomplished.

* Tell how it happened, and where and when it took place.

* Include a quotation telling how you feel about reaching your goal.

63

# Acting Across Generations

**EVANSTON, ILLINOIS** When the Evanston Children's Theatre decided to put on a play of *Charlotte's Web*, they invited kids from eight to twelve years old to try out for parts. They asked seniors age 55 and older to try out, too. Usually, child actors wear gray wigs and paste on fake beards and moustaches to look old. This group uses real seniors.

A few years ago, the Evanston city council decided that the children's theater would have its home in the Levy Center, Evanston's new senior center. So it just seemed natural to get both the kids and the seniors working together.

This experiment has worked well for several plays. Kids play most parts. It's a children's theater group, after all. But seniors have one or two roles in each play.

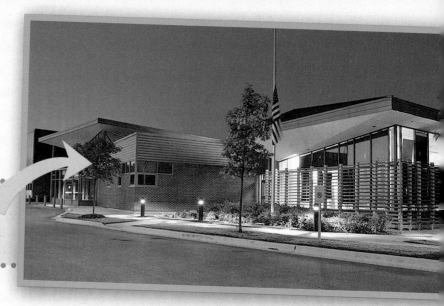

**The Evanston Children's Theatre**

The Levy Center holds different senior classes. Seniors who take acting classes try out for the children's theater. Working with kids keeps seniors young. Working with seniors helps kids, too. The seniors share tips from their acting classes, and the kids show what they've learned.

To put on a play, actors must help one another. If a senior forgets some lines, kids jump right in and move the scene along. Seniors do the same for the kids. Once a senior got sick after the first show. A kid took on the senior's part. The show must go on—and it did!

Putting on plays is great fun, but the Evanston Children's Theatre gives seniors and kids a chance to help one another. Bravo!

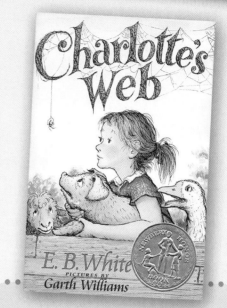

The Evanston Children's Theatre has become very popular. In fact, more than 300 people came to a Sunday afternoon performance of *Charlotte's Web.*

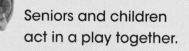

Seniors and children act in a play together.

65

# SAVING BUSTER

"Go get it, boy!" Mrs. Parker yelled as she tossed Buster's favorite ball across the yard. Donovan Lowe was pulling weeds in the Parkers' front yard. He watched Buster streak by and smiled. Donovan liked Mrs. Parker. A year ago she'd had a stroke. That's when she moved in with her daughter Liz, Donovan's neighbor.

The stroke left Mrs. Parker weak enough to need a wheelchair, but it didn't affect her funny bone. Everyone loved her jokes and stories. She was like the whole neighborhood's grandmother. Buster was her service dog, and he was like the whole neighborhood's pet.

He raced back with the ball.

"Okay!" Mrs. Parker laughed. "But this is the last time! I'm exhausted!"

Mrs. Parker threw the ball again. It bounced and rolled into the street. At that exact moment, a truck swung around the corner. There was no way the driver could stop in time.

"*Buuuussss-terrrrr!*" both Donovan and Mrs. Parker shouted. Donovan sped to the curb where Buster lay. The truck driver was kneeling beside the dog.

"Get a blanket and call the vet!" he yelled to Donovan. "Tell them it's an emergency, and we're on our way!"

That night Donovan and his mom brought her tortilla casserole over to the Parkers. Liz reported what the vet had told them. "Dr. Sims thinks that Buster will need to go to the animal hospital in the city for an operation. She'll call tomorrow when she knows more."

The next morning, Donovan waited nervously for news about Buster. Around ten o'clock, Liz called. Donovan stayed near until his mother hung up. "Buster has two broken legs," his mom said. "The doctors will operate today. You and I will help out with Mrs. Parker while Liz is at the animal hospital."

Donovan and Mrs. Parker looked at old photo albums while they waited for Liz. They shared funny stories about Buster. Donovan's mom did what she always did in times of stress. She cooked.

Liz returned late that evening. Buster would have casts on his legs for a while, but he'd be all right.

Mrs. Parker and Donovan played a game as his mother heated some food for Liz. Then Donovan went into the kitchen to get a glass of water. Mom and Liz were washing dishes and didn't hear him come in.

"We don't have two thousand dollars to pay for Buster's care!" Liz exclaimed. "I don't know how we'll ever pay it."

Donovan slipped back into the living room. He had $17 he had saved for a new computer game. He'd give it to Liz, but Liz needed two thousand dollars. What else could he do?

That night, Donovan told his mom what he had overheard. "I want to help, but I don't know how."

Mom said softly, "It's a big problem, honey. Sleep on it. Maybe in the morning, we'll have an idea."

No brilliant idea came to Donovan during the night. Nor did one come during school the next day. When he got home, his mom was testing a new recipe. "Taste this, please," she said as she held a spoonful of stew under his nose.

Donovan cleaned the spoon and declared, "Delicious! You should have a cooking show."

"Thank you! I made enough for Liz and Mrs. Parker too. Would you carry it over for me?" Mom asked.

Liz was on the phone as she answered the door. She pointed Donovan to the kitchen. "Just put it anywhere," she whispered as she turned back to her phone conversation.

Donovan stared at the counters. It seemed as if all their neighbors had sent food. Donovan squeezed his bowl in between two dishes. Then he stopped to see how Mrs. Parker was holding up.

"I'm fine, but it's hard on Liz. She has to do everything that Buster used to do for me."

And worry about how she's going to pay the vet bill, Donovan thought.

"What did your mom send over?" Mrs. Parker asked.

"Stew," said Donovan. "But I think you have a wide menu to choose from tonight. I haven't seen that many dishes since the school's potluck supper."

Mrs. Parker whispered, "I know. But your mom's the best cook around."

Donovan smiled. He thought so too. As he walked home, that brilliant idea he'd been waiting for started brewing in his head. As his thoughts sped up, so did his feet.

Donovan burst into the kitchen and announced, "I know how to pay for Buster's operation! We'll have a potluck cooking contest! People can pay to enter. They'll make a sample of food for the judges to taste and a large pot for people to eat. Then people can pay to eat the food!"

The more his mother and Donovan talked, the more excited they became. People could buy tickets for $2 each. Each ticket would pay for a helping from a pot they wanted to taste.

Ideas flowed quickly after that. They'd have cooking contests for adults and for kids. Someone could sell pictures of people and their pets. Others could demonstrate what service dogs do. They could even have a Funniest-Looking Pet contest. They would call it the Pet Potluck Fair. Mrs. Lowe checked with Liz, Mrs. Parker, and some neighbors. Everyone loved their idea.

The day of the potluck contest came. Friends and neighbors filled the park. Buster was the guest of honor. He sat in a special wagon next to Mrs. Parker. Donovan helped sell food tickets. Liz took pictures of people with their pets. Mrs. Parker and Buster judged the pet contest. A bulldog was chosen the funniest-looking pet. It wasn't a surprise when Donovan's mom won the cooking contest. But the best moment came at the end of the day.

Carl Baca was a banker who lived on Donovan's street. He made a special announcement. "Buster has shown us how important a service dog can be. Because we care, we've raised more than one thousand dollars toward Buster's vet bill!" The crowd hollered and clapped.

Donovan hollered and clapped too, but he knew that it wasn't enough. Liz was about to thank the crowd when Mr. Baca held up a hand. "When Donovan Lowe talked to me about raising money for Buster, I made a vow. I told myself that my bank would do all it could to help raise this money. I talked to other businesses in our neighborhood too. And we will make up the difference. We will donate the rest of the money needed to pay Buster's vet bill."

The crowd hollered and clapped even more. Liz laughed and cried at the same time. So did Mrs. Lowe and Mrs. Parker. Buster looked up at Donovan. Donovan could have sworn Buster was smiling. And that was all the thanks Donovan needed.

# Company's Coming!

David L. Harrison

What a mess!
A total wreck!
They're nearly here!
All hands on deck!

Clear the table!
Grab the shoes!
Make the beds!
No time to lose!

Cram the closets!
Slam the doors!
Hang the jackets!
Mop the floors!

Shove those socks
And underwear
And magazines
Beneath a chair!

Faster! Faster!
Not enough!
Move it! Shake it!
Hide this stuff!

Get some crackers
On a plate!
Pray that they
Are running late!

Slice the cheese!
Put out the cat!
Someone check
That thermostat!

Change the soap
And wipe the tile!
We're all sweaty!

Ding Dong!

Smile!

**Discuss Poetry**
What patterns of rhymes and beats can you find in this poem? How are lines divided? How do the exclamation points make the poem sound and feel?

# Make a Poster

You read the story.
Now come see the play!

## Charlotte's Web

Charlotte and Wilbur and all their friends on stage!

For three days only
Friday, Saturday, and Sunday
October 12-14
7:00 p.m.

**Story Theater**
**2525 West Main Street**

Tickets on sale at the theater now!

This poster does two things: it grabs your attention and gives information.

Make a poster of your own. Think of an event you would want people to come to. It could be a play, a race, a bake sale, or a fun fair. Plan what you will put on your poster and how you will grab people's attention. Then start writing and drawing.

# One Plus One ...Equals One!

It's not math, but when it comes to making words, one plus one can equal one. A **compound word** is one word made up of two smaller words.

**Example:**

grand + mother = grandmother

On a sheet of paper, use the picture clues to make a compound word from two small words. The words in the box below are in the compound words you will write. Some words are used twice.

## Words Used

boat

drum

pin

chair

ear

stick

dog

house

wheel

1. + = _____?_____

2. + = _____?_____

3. + = _____?_____

4. + = _____?_____

5. + = _____?_____

6. + = _____?_____

## The Fair Needs

Often a big problem like Buster's accident takes many people to help solve it. A fair is a fun way to solve a problem. Think of a problem that you would like to help solve by holding a fair. Maybe your school playground needs more equipment. Maybe a local pet shelter needs a bigger building. Write a letter to a newspaper to persuade other people to help you put on a fair. Give reasons that are right for your audience, and use persuasive words. Write with a confident tone.

- Explain the problem.
- Give reasons why people should help.
- Describe the kind of fair you want to hold.
- Tell exactly what your readers can do to help.

YOU!

# Credits

## Photo Credits

**KEY**: (t) top, (b) bottom, (l) left, (r) right, (c) center, (bg) background, (fg) foreground, (i) inset

Cover (bg) Bobby Model/National Geographic Society; (cl) Colin Young-Wolff/Photo Edit; (bl) Mike Kemp/Getty Images; Title Page (bg) Didrik Johnck/Corbis; (t) AP Photo/United States Postal Service; 1 (bl) AP Photo/United States Postal Service; (br) F. Lukasseck/Masterfile; (br) AP Photo/United States Postal Service; (bc) AP Photo/United States Postal Service; (tr) Bettmann/Corbis; (tl) Suzanna Price/Getty Images; 2 (bl) Comstock Images/Getty Images; 3 (tr) Alex Wong/Getty Images; 4 (b) F. Lukasseck/Masterfile; (bg) PhotoDisc, Inc./Getty Images; (t) Barbara Strnadova/ Photo Researchers, Inc.; (b) Carol Farneti Foster/Getty Images; 6 (l) Bettmann/Corbis; 7 (b) Bettmann/Corbis; 8 (b) Bettmann/Corbis; 10 (b) © James Steinberg / Photo Researchers, Inc.; 11 (t) Underwood & Underwood/Corbis; 12 (br) Tom Strattman/Getty Images; 13 (br) dk/Alamy; (bl) Ilene MacDonald/Alamy; 15 (bg) Dynamic Graphics/Jupiterimages/ Getty Images; (bg) Alamy; 16 (all) AP Photo/United States Postal Service; 21 (bl) Suzanna Price/Getty Images; (tr) Colin Young-Wolff/Photo Edit; 22 (bl) sciencephotos/Alamy; (br) sciencephotos/Alamy; (tr) Michal Newman/PhotoEdit; 23 (tr) Hulton-Deutsch Collection/Corbis; (b) © Paul Rapson / Photo Researchers, Inc.; 24 (b) Lester Lefkowitz/Corbis; 25 (br) Hemera/AgeFotostock; (tr) Don Farrall/PhotoDisc/Getty Images; 26 (b) Thomas Michael Corcoran/PhotoEdit; (b) Astra Production/Picture Press/PhotoLibrary; 27 (bl) Matthias Kulka/zefa/Corbis; (c) Corbis; 32 (b) Dennis MacDonald/Alamy; 33 (b) Frank Boxler/AP Images; (t) Brian Kersey/AP Images; 34 Didrik Johnck/Corbis; 36 (bg) PhotoDisc/GettyImages; 37 (cr) altrendo images/Getty Images; (tr) imagebroker/Alamy; 38 (fg) PhotoDisc/GettyImages; (r) Didrik Johnck/Corbis; (l) Gavin Attwood/Touch the Top; 42 (bg) Photodisc, Inc/Getty Images; Comstock Images/Getty Images; 43 (r) Rudi Von Briel/PhotoEdit; 44 (b) image100/Alamy; 46 (b) Michael A. Keller/Corbis; 56 (b) Jeff Hutchens/Getty Images; (t) Alex Wong/Getty Images; 57 (b) Chip Somodevilla/Getty Images; 58 (bg) David Young-Wolff; 59 Digital Vision/Alamy; 64 (b) Bill Nesius; 65 (b) Paul Barton/Corbis; 79 (bl) i love images/Alamy; (cr) Steve Warmowski/The Image Works; (br) Mary Ellen Bartley/Getty Images.

All other photos are property of Houghton Mifflin Harcourt.